CERTAINTY

CERTAINTY

POEMS BY DAVID ROMTVEDT

WHITE PINE PRESS • FREDONIA, NEW YORK

ACKNOWLEDGEMENTS:
American Poetry Review: Ultimate Nightingale; Wyoming I Do Not Own
Borderlands: My Poem; My Shovel; It's Funny (as Having a Rest)
Casper Star-Tribune: The Ice; Politics; Unbelievable
Crab Creek Review's World Voice Anthology: Becoming a Poet
Cutbank: This Year's Wood
Dakotah: Books
Event: My Art; An English Country Cottage; The Rose Bushes; My Father's Death
The Guadalupe Review: The End of the Century; Once Upon a Time
The Journal: The Biggest Fish
Kumquat Meringue: Halloween
The Missouri Review: My Flame; My Porch; My Wife; Painting the Fence; The Radio;
        Welcome; Windows
Pivot: Ho Chi Minh City
Ploughshares: Who Owes Us
Poetry East: Iris
Portrait: The Poetry of Love
The Sun: Another Saigon Intersection; Autonomy; Deep Blue Flower; My Daughter's
        Room; My Death; My Father and the Buddha; My Job; My Village; My
        Winter Wood; This Time of War; Traffic
Willow Springs: Spring Cleaning; Planting

"Welcome" was published by Ion Books and Black Cedar Press as a limited edi-
tion broadside.

Publication of this book was made possible, in part,
by grants from the National Endowment for the Arts
and the New York State Council on the Arts.

Cover Painting: Dollie Iberlin

ISBN 1-877727-59-8

Manufactured in the United States of America

Printed on recycled paper

White Pine Press • 10 Village Square • Fredonia, New York 14063

for Margo

CONTENTS

CERTAINTY

WELCOME

Strangers do not wish to hear of a stranger's life.
Houses have walls to keep them apart. The interstate
highway skirts the edge of town in a great looping curve.
The drivers pass one another with windows rolled up
and music playing loudly. When the weather is unbearably
sweet, the neighbors come out and sit alone in their yards,
basking in the sun and enjoying drinks made cold with ice.
It is lovely. I stand and walk through the alleys,
amidst the spilled garbage cans, the oilspots in the dust,
the birds and squirrels torn apart by domestic cats,
the old Jeeps propped up on blocks. One woman has built
a fence around her garden and hanging from it are onions
drying in the sun, hundreds of white globes, large as
grapefruit. They smell strong as trees with their tops
spilled over and mottled brown and green. I want to tell
the gardener what pleasure they give me so I step through
the yard and knock on the back door. "Excuse me," I practice,
"I was passing and..." Or, "Hello, I live down the block..."
Or, "Your onions! They..." I knock again but no one comes.
I leave, looking once more at the fence and the onions
inviting me to bend and touch them in caress.

MY JOB

I have been dreaming, but I cannot remember my dream.
I can explain—I work hard every day and at night
fall into the sleep of a log or stone, silent and still.
In this dream everything is clear—my work, my marriage
and children, my daily greetings to my neighbors,
the feelings I have when told we have successfully
tested another weapon of mass destruction. I set
the alarm and in the morning get up to eat. I am happy
swallowing oatmeal with raisins and walnuts and
I am happy walking out the door to work and I am
happy when the sky darkens and the rain tumbles down.
That's funny, I think to myself, the way the rain strikes
the ground or my head and it is the same plink, plink,
everywhere it falls, the same plink, plink, plink.

PLANTING

I get up early and go to work in the garden.
The neighbors are asleep and the streets are quiet.
I crumble the cool dark moist earth, making it fine,
then I plant the seeds. A few birds quit singing
and fly down from the hedge to watch. I explain
what I'm doing, slightly ashamed to be revealing
the secrets of the universe. Maybe I'm withholding
them. Sometimes the birds cock their heads and listen
to the entire talk. Sometimes they fly away while
I'm in mid-sentence. "Wait," I call out, "This
is the origin of life on earth." The neighbor
rushes out of his house, letting the back door slam.
He dives into his car and turns the key in the ignition.
Gunning the motor, he grins devilishly and races away
to his job at the metal fabricating shop. We wave goodbye
to each other. As the car disappears down the street,
I return to my carrots, beans, basil and corn, hoping
I got the seeds in right. If they're planted too deep,
it's like being buried and they'll never come up.

ULTIMATE NIGHTINGALE

My ultimate nightingale—vivid, doubtful, whistling in a whisper.
The past zings by me like an automobilist making up lost time.

A quart of water—not such a grand thing, not so clear
as it once was, still clear enough to let the light pass.

Electricity—even in a cafe alone I can feel it,
the blood of the city coursing after the power goes out.

This is the tango—I put one foot here and lead you
where you'd planned to go. The tango is beautiful and vile.

The earth has sealed itself from us—mouth sealed,
eyes sealed, anus, fingertips, ears, heart, all sealed, from us.

A blue vase—pale as some skies, or the egg of a bird,
or a lover's touch from across a wide bed and then together.

There are mysteries in the world—thoughts and moments, salmon,
rivers, rain, the leisure that surrounds us day after day.

FLOWERS

There is a mattress on the living room floor
and an oxygen tank on wheels beside the piano.
The sun rising, here comes my daughter now, slowly
moving down the birth canal toward early morning light.
Her mother and I are on our hands and knees facing
one another. Our cheeks and ears touch. She is leaning
forward, pushing with all her strength, her nose pressed
into my collarbone. She cries out and clamps down, biting
deeply into the flesh at the base of my neck. The tears
from her eyes run down my cheek. Weeks later she told me
she was in terrible pain and yet not. "Yes," I said, "Once
in an accident, my finger was cut off and I didn't know it
until I tried to use my hand." "No, not like that," she said.
"Well, once, I drove an electric drill through the soft part
of my hand. When I pulled the bit out, I felt faint."
"Maybe the feeling faint," she allowed. But now the baby
has come. Her hair is black and matted on her head. One ear
is crushed, like a fluted mushroom. She rests against her mother
who rests on the floor. "Look," my tired wife says, smiling,
"at your shoulder." There are red teeth marks, a jagged circle
of blood. "It looks like a rose," she laughs and when we turn,
we see the room is brilliant, overflowing with flowers.

My Flame

My finger rests motionless for a moment above the flame,
then I jerk it away. It is painful. Do any of those
thin men in India really walk across beds of coals?
I pull my cigarette from my mouth and watch the smoke
pour away from me, the heat running to get as far as it can
from my body. I flick the ash and touch the glowing ember
to the soft skin on my forearm. That hurts, too. I can
burn the hair on the back of my arm. It curls and stinks,
leaving my arm smooth and pale. The hair is me but does
not hurt. The skin hurts a great deal. This time I press
the burning cigarette hard into the skin. My eyes water.
I press it again and again—both forearms, my cheeks, three
dark holes under my eyes, I am burning myself in small ways.
How do those men do it? Not the Indians but the monks, those
Buddhists, those Vietnamese. One man sat down in the center
of a Saigon street. A second man, a fellow monk, poured
gasoline over the first who then carefully set a burning
match against his faded orange robes. The flames shot forth,
knocking people off the sidewalk, knocking the second monk
down, knocking the Swedish rifle I carry out of my arms.
The flames shoot farther, hotter, brighter, shoot to Heaven.

I Couldn't Wait

I couldn't wait for you. Driving, I hit a child on a bike.
At the hospital, I wished this world was not the way it is.

You told me life is hell, but sometimes it's heaven.
You laughed and pretended to put a gun to your head.

I plant both annual and perennial flowers, some to bloom
in spring and some in fall. Still, one day there are none.

My son is grown with a son of his own. I am shamed
by the father I was, he by himself as son.

People whine because they are dying too soon, or because
they are living too long. They could be God or a housefly.

Panting in the heat, the dog stares at a patch of shade.
Covered with snow, the leaf bends toward the ground.

I know the difference between an elegy and a requiem.
There is the phone ringing now.

My Shovel

I drive down a straight wide road for miles.
When I reach the mall flooded with light
I turn in and stop the car. The building
is shining there across a parking lot
large enough to be a farm. I take the key
and open the trunk, lifting from the dark
cavity a shovel I carry in case of winter
emergency on the road. I begin to dig
but the asphalt is cold and hard and
the mall lights have gone out and the end
of my shovel is blunt. I return the shovel
to the trunk then bend over to inspect
the crack I have made in the asphalt,
certain that there in that space is the image
of a cemetery rising on a grassy slope.
I bend down to my hands and knees and peel
back a little more of the asphalt. I see
that I was mistaken—there is no cemetery,
there is only one stone, bearing my name.

MY FATHER AND THE BUDDHA

I go to the library with my questions.
It never occurs to me to ask my father.
I look up Buddhism and ask the Buddha.
The page is dim. The Buddha grins,
no answer of any kind, more questions.
After my father's death I ask him
about this. He has never heard of the Buddha
and tells me he suspects religion of any kind.
Not religion so much as men claiming religion—
talking about it or preaching or doing things
to other men and women. First, they drop water
on a child, they place a wafer on a youth's tongue,
they offer wine to an old man. "These are Catholic
rites," I say. "It's what I know," my father
says. "First these, then the next thing, you turn
around, they've started a war and millions are dead."
"Not the Buddhists," I claim. "They rarely
start wars." My father wonders if this could be
true. He leans on his hand and looks out the window
onto the Sonora Desert where I grew up, the saguaro
cactus and ocotillo and sunbathing snakes. A smile
spreads across his broad face. I turn to see
what has happened and am surprised that my father
is outside shoveling deep snow off the warm earth.

Wyoming I Do Not Own

Winter is so long! It is not as though we are snowed
in. We are wintered in. On September 9 it was twenty
degrees and all the plants in the garden but parsley
died. Black tomato vines tumbled down to mush, and
eggplant and beans, the parsley sparkling green, a noisy
cheer. Then cold and wind and the dark growing
each day, night overwhelming the day until December 3
when it began to snow and snowed for three days, forty
inches in all. We built a snow hut and dug paths to get
from the house to the compost pit to the studio to the
sheep wagon. All of January, then February, March
and, unyieldingly, April. In May I hammered my way
into the earth, digging a trench for a gas line.
As I dug, the wind cut through me and the snow fell,
May 9, May 10, May 11, until May 12 when the sun
shone and it was hot and winter ended. It did?
Winter is not winter. The blue sky draws me up
to Cloud Peak. I have forgotten my skis and so tuck
my hands in my pockets, curl up in a ball and roll
down the mountain to town where I rise from my slide
at my back door. I touch the knob. It is cold!
I knock and when the door opens, walk on in.

MY PLANET

It is lonely thinking that among the uncounted planets
mine is the only one glowing with life. Still, I love
this time of seclusion. In the early morning I walk
to the outhouse up the hillside on the winding path.
The little valley below me is filled with fog that rises
like smoke from human fires through the trees. I step
around a corner and see a pile of bearshit on the trail.
Steam rising, it seems to laugh at me and my outhouse.
In the late afternoon I take the lid from the black
trash can where I store water. The sun has warmed it.
I scoop some out to wash my face and neck, my underarms.
On summer days like these the birds and crickets sing,
the flies buzz, the deer stand still in the grass. This
is Heaven and I want to tell those distant beings, so
I turn and dance and wave and smile and shout and breathe.
I don't know if anyone notices. Though I am large, even
the closest planet is far away and busy with its own spin.

What is Money?

The ice on the lake is several feet thick.
In the cold water, out of sight, the fish swim.

It feels good to ask philosophical questions
while eating popcorn, my lips smeared with butter.

Deaf, blind, tottering and frail, my hundred year old
grandmother licks cake frosting off her fingers.

Don't talk to me about time. Your goddam lecture
seems to be taking a million years to end.

Complain, complain, complain! If this were the twelfth
century, we'd be standing in line to buy hair shirts.

The magician of nature—lightning strikes a robin's egg,
a raven bursts into flame and the robin flies away.

I sit still on the porch. A butterfly lands on my nose
and rests there. I have to cross my eyes in order to see.

IRIS

I transplanted iris bulbs along the wall of the garage,
almost in the alley. No one can see them there except
the garbagemen as they fling cans in and out of their truck.
The neighbor says they're so thick it's a wonder they can bloom.
Hundreds of deep purple blossoms, the purple vibrating against
the green stalks and leaves, the pale blue wall of the building.
Even the air around the flowers shimmers and clings. The hose
won't reach so I haul water in a bucket, again and again,
standing, watching the water rise then walking carefully,
lopsided, a little water splashing out onto my legs as I go.
The Buddhist monks stand in lines—long lines going back
row after row, deep human. They slide forward, barely
lifting their soft feet from the ground. Facing them,
at the end of the muddy street, are the police, in helmets,
with guns, or soldiers, or members of the rubber workers
union, or brothers and sisters of civil servants, or students
from the university that has been closed, everyone dressed
in neat black pants and white shirts, and there are the monks,
shaved heads bobbing on thin necks. Before the crowd, they stop
and sit down in the road. I can smell the sweat from beneath
their arms and the perfume that saturates their spotless robes.

RECREATION

I run and run and run even though my knee hurts
so much that there are tears in my eyes. My lungs
clatter around in my chest like two songbirds
who've flown in an open window and cannot find
their way out. Soon they will die unless someone
captures them and carefully carries them outside.
I open my hands and there are two tiny eggs,
pale green with soft peach colored speckles.
My dog bounds from the porch, hurling his body
through the air and colliding with me, knocking me
to the ground where I crush the eggs. The birds
explode from my mouth, mucous and blood drying
on their wings as they deliberately careen away.

SWINGING

The hammock hangs low over the mint plants.
As I swing, the leaves tickle my shoulders and neck.

The days are hot. Each afternoon the clouds pile up
and it looks as if it will rain, but it doesn't.

I was told I'd won a great honor. It turned out to be
a mistake and now, though my life is the same, I am sad.

The paper reports a sixth Soviet Republic has seceded
from the union. Here they vow to make Puerto Rico a state.

There are nine lizards climbing my wall. Each is silent
with a red tail and a flashing pink tongue.

No matter how long you polish clay, it won't be a mirror.
There's my reflection now.

In the middle of a conversation with my mother, my father's face
floats into sight. I tell him I forgot what I meant to say.

MY HISTORY

This is my snowy mountain, and these are my dark trees.
I can hold the cold in my hand and not freeze.
The raw wind is a brother's greeting. The gray clouds
are the ever longer book of my breath, chapter on chapter,
filling the sky. Today I notice because I am not alone.
I am helping another man learn to ski—showing him how
the gator fits over his boot, how the strap of his pole
slides under his palm, how his left ski can be told from
his right, how to walk and turn and stop. He is a Pala
from San Diego. The city fills the land his people once knew.
He is dark and squat with a wide face. His neck is as big
as my thigh. When we set off, he falls. When we climb
he slips and stumbles. Sweat rolls down his face
and freezes on his cheeks. His body jerks as he tries
to glide when he pushes forward, favoring his right side.
He has never been on skis. It is twenty-five thousand years
since his people came to California. In the early years
of this century my grandfather left Norway for Minnesota
then Texas then Oregon. The sigh I release gathers into
a large cloud. The winter sun sets and the cold envelops
us. Pride and shame and happiness and anger ricochet off
the trees. So does the wind making the snow fall.

My Companion

How far away is summer—those long days of sun and heat!
They seem mysterious and impossible now in the dark and cold.
Just the past made of emotions and desire. I take off my glove
and jam my hand deep into the newly fallen snow, shearing off
the edge of the pack and exposing the layers of change—the new
crystals with their sharp edges, the old ones rounded and worn,
the avalanche layer like ball bearings waiting to roll. Some
old Chinese poet would say there is beauty all around, then
raise his wine glass to the winter moon. In the pale light
I recognize the old guy—he falls face first into the snow
and it's up to me to pick him up gently and carry him home.

My Winter Wood

My winter wood has been stacked for months, drying
in the summer sun. On this northern desert there is no rain,
nearly no dew. When winter comes, the snow is so cold
that no water can enter the wood. Gloveless, I brush
the dry powder from atop the stack. There is neither
roof nor walls to protect it. Squirrels run in and out
of the pile and neighborhood children struggle to pull
a few thin pieces out and use them as swords or guns.
No one has ever stolen any of my wood but I like to believe
one could. If a person were really cold he could step quietly
under cover of night through my gate and into my silent yard.
There is the wood! Bits of bark lie dark on the white snow.
My visitor's boots crackle as he walks. By the woodpile
is a wheelbarrow. Whoever is there slowly lifts each morsel
and sets it down in the cart. When the wood touches the metal
there is a ringing as of a bell, but softly so that,
though I hear, I only smile slightly and turn in my sleep.

This Morning

Day or night, it is morning thoughout the universe.
In the kitchen the glittering nebula and silent vacuum.

I work in a factory. I hammer metal. Several times a day
I sweep silvery shavings off the wooden floor.

This rayon shirt is soft and the colors are so brilliant
I have to shade my eyes—circles and triangles and squares.

The yard is filled with young trees—spruce, aspen, juniper,
birch and ash. I want to plant more but there isn't any room.

This is the sixth year of drought. The creek continues low,
the rocks rising into the sky, the muddy banks turning to dust.

When my father died I felt dizzy and confused. When I turned
my head, it took a moment for the world to turn with it.

The car is out of gas. We push and discover the wheels roll.
The northern desert rushes toward us and the scent of sage.

BARCELONA

Yesterday I realized I had forgotten Barcelona—not only the
word, but the city itself and all those who live there.
Now I remember the flower vendor and the kosher butcher
on the Street of the Infant Martyrs. I remember a small boy
dragging his bright blue nylon pack through the dust
as he runs toward school. Turning a corner I nearly collide
with a pretty woman who is walking out of a shop. She smiles
at me and her magenta dress bristles like flame. I am so
excited I clap my hands and the pigeons rise from the wet
gutters like clouds of dark diesel rolling up along the walls
of the ancient buildings. I want to keep this forever—this
place I might never see again, these foreign words and that
sky whose blue is strange. Such longing! And I can neither
hold on to it nor really let it go.

PAINTING THE FENCE

I was going to say I thought of that monk again,
the one burning himself to death in Saigon. But
the truth is I did not think of him, I saw him.
The monk is dead but the smallest thing brings him home.
I am painting the fence beside the garden. First I scrape
the old paint away. Huge flakes fall from the boards
and land in the dirt. Then I spread the new paint
on the raw boards. Drops of oil-based primer mottle
the leaves of lettuce at my feet. Finished, I walk
to the garage and unscrew the lid to the gasoline
I use as paint thinner. The odor fills my nose. As if
a burning match had been thrown into my open mouth,
I gulp it down and choke. I cough again and again,
hacking, trying to pull up whatever is blocking my breath.
Here is the monk, pounding me on the back, assuring me
I'll be fine, this is my grandest moment, wrapped in
smoke, my hands waving flames as tears roll down my face.

An English Country Cottage

When we found our house, it was painted a sickly yellow green.
Busy with what we called life, we left it alone for years.
Finally, one May, we worked for weeks, our baby daughter lying
in the grass at our feet. We repainted the house a creamy delicate
blue, the color of a songbird's egg. The trim, we repainted white
with fine red lines. Looking at the changed house, we knew it held
an embryo, growing. First the baby would hatch and, then, fly.
"It's charming!" people said. "Like an English Country Cottage."
I pictured narrow winding lanes with tall hedges, long leaved
chestnut trees, neatly cultivated fields, and flowers everywhere—
roses, dahlias, chrysanthemums. But this is Wyoming and, though it's
only October, the temperature last night was twelve below zero.
It has been snowing for days. The tops of the mountains are buried
in heavy jagged clouds and the draws are filled with drifting, blowing
snow. Excited and anxious, I pull on layers of clothing, wear wool
socks under my light running shoes and set off in the dark, following
the edges of the slick roads. In a neighborhood in the middle of
town, I surprise a deer who leaps in front of me, slips on the icy
street, and bounds across someone's front yard, running in front
of a large picture window. For a moment the deer shimmers in the
glow from the house. Inside, a woman talking on the telephone drops
the receiver, runs to the window and presses her face to the cold
glass. But the deer is gone so all she sees is me—a heavily bundled
man—running by and the large puff of breath rising from my mouth.

My Daughter's Room

My daughter lies sick in bed. I pace across the small room,
rubbing my hands together while she tosses and groans in pain,
her hair stuck to her head that is hot with fever, her eyes
cloudy and far away. Outside, the snow melts on the fence
as if nothing had ever changed and never would. A few eager
birds have returned north too soon and a few blades of grass
have sprung up among last fall's dead growth. In her room,
my daughter's presence, like that of the universe, goes on
forever and is filled with stars. As I reach the light, one
star recedes and another winks into sight. In this blink
of time, I bend and brush her arm. She opens her eyes
and my dead father looks out, his smile both wan and sly.

DEED

Here is the deed to my house and land.
I own my car, too, free and clear.

Flying to the moon requires a rocket ship.
I'm looking through the catalogues for one on sale.

When I was young these hills were bare and brown.
Now the apartments rise, closer each day to the sky.

Please don't talk to me about world events.
I'm dressing for a party and I'm already late.

This suit just came back from the cleaners. Hey,
there's a grease spot and blobs of dried blood.

My father-in-law says I should break down and get a TV.
There are some good things on it and everyone has one.

Here's someone's finger that was cut off in an accident.
The doctors sew it to my hand and, presto, it's mine.

My Poem

I've borrowed this poem and cannot return it.
Puzzled, I watch the shadow move far from my body.
The sky is clear because the clouds are gone.
A starling's jagged song bursts from a tree
followed by a gunshot. When I sleep at night
I do not fret over the floating world. Sometimes
I remember my dreams and sometimes I do not.
I remember the one about the mountain and the cabin
on fire, but not the one about the flower. My son
and daughter play in the yard, filling it with noise
and time. There's the phone. I hope I don't forget
what I want to say. It's a call from a thief to whom
I have given writing lessons. Convicted, he awaits
his release from jail, unaware that his crime
is a capital one. In the interim he is writing poems.
He wants to know if they are any good. I tell him yes.
It doesn't matter if they are good or bad, but yes
they are good. He is angry. I explain that no one
takes pity on you simply because you commit a crime.
The priest has come to give him the last rites.
He is not a Catholic and his crime was to steal
gourmet food. He had lived on food stamps
and was ashamed to buy imported artichoke hearts
and fresh blueberries. He wanted to take pleasure
in eating when his food stamps had been meant only to
keep him alive. He waves the priest away, saying,
"I am busy writing a poem." Then he tells me he has
been saving his one phone call for me. "This is it,
then?" I ask. "Yes." he says, and the line goes dead.

My Wife

I am my wife's husband. I belong to her. When we part
for a day, it takes another to catch up on our talk.
When we look at our daughter, we smile and hold each
other in our arms. Before our meals the three of us
pause. We do not say a prayer or any words at all.
We hold hands and look in each others' eyes. Sometimes
we look out the window next to our table. A squirrel
runs along the top of our fence. Our daughter forgets
us for a moment and says, "Squirrel." Then we eat.
We stuff ourselves full of beauty and ugliness, and
right and wrong and, for picnics, bread and cheese.
On these outings we play volleyball and talk philosophy.
The Buddhists say, "All things are impermanent." That
makes us laugh. Because it is true, and true, too, that
we are in love forever and everything is here to stay.

WEEKEND

All day each day I worked at the ski pole factory
while outside it was one hundred degrees and the leaves
on the trees fell limp in the heat. On Saturday
I rose early and walked far into the mountains.
At 10,000 feet I set up my tent. Peak upon peak
surrounded me, rising higher and higher into the sky.
Also, other tents and campers and pickups. Smoke
rose from fires, and portable tape recorders sang
recent songs from California. I brewed strong tea
in a charred pot then moved away out of the smoke
to sit alone. The milky clouds filled the sky
and inside a great herd of whales crossed the sea.

AUTONOMY

Now at three my daughter answers every question
beginning with "Would you...?" by saying, "No."
And every gesture I make toward her she considers
an act of aggression. She is fierce in defense
of her integrity while reminding me many times
each day that, "I love you, Dad." And I understand.
I love her, too, and would stand aside as, like a flower,
she blooms. When I was ten, my father made me sit
outside in full view of the neighbors and play German polkas
on the piano accordion. It was hot and both my body
and the large black musical instrument became slick
with sweat. I tried to play quietly, fantastically
hoping no one would hear, and my father screamed,
"Louder, play louder." I felt I could not bear
my embarrassment and impotence, my father's complete
power over me. Yet I did bear it. I bore it as I had to.
Such a small thing! To play the accordion for one's father.
But it was not small. Those moments of childhood return,
and my stomach is a dense knot of hatred and shame.
My sad father, wanting happiness and ease, shaking
with exhaustion when he came home from his labor,
calling me to bring the accordion outside and play
while he rested and I bitterly did so, and he knew.
But he could not change it, could save neither
himself nor me. So you see how it is that I am elated
when my daughter says no again, her voice a single petal
that I must not try to catch as it tumbles to the ground.

This Time of War

On the birthday of Dr. Martin Luther King the United States
bombed the people of Iraq. A great man. We remember.

My friend's beautiful sister wears a diamond nose ring,
not at all like the heavy iron ring in the nose of a bull.

Here the shaman sits with his drum and his eyes on Heaven.
They say when the drum dies so too the shaman. Not true.

All the world is a bomb shelter that does not work. Shhh!
The trees do not know. Nor the birds and grasses. The earth.

I yelled at my wife and daughter. I cursed the frozen bolts,
cutting them off to put a new muffler on the car I needn't drive.

I'm eating ice cream and cookies and drinking licorice tea.
Rich foods I eat so rarely. Now seems the right time.

There is a stone wall that rises in the door to my bedroom
each night. Each morning I tear it down and enter the day.

The Radio

On the radio I hear the voice of a friend who once
lived with us here on Piney Creek. Now in the city
she reports on matters of the soul, of childhood, of
Norwegian immigrants, of widows who are alone and sad,
of oranges and Christmas, of the way we go on making
war after war. She remembers her brother Jerome, a
skinny kid who joined the army and died in Vietnam,
and how the night he left she was so angry she couldn't
say goodbye. Maybe if this, maybe if that—Jerome would
never have joined the army and so today would not be dead,
mother and father not stare darkly at one another,
each unsure who the other might be, sister would not
work at a job she hates, there would be no more war.
My friend says that every time she talks to someone
or puts a word down on paper, she asks herself,
"Will this open up a heart? Would it make a bird sing?"
And hearing her beautiful human voice, there is a tug
inside my chest and tears fill my eyes even though I know
nothing will open a closed heart but the heart itself.
And in Vietnam, the birds whistled and shrieked and what
we did made them neither start nor stop if they chose to sing.

It's Funny

These are the moments, ticking.
Only I don't own a watch.

We are walking together through the forest.
It's muddy and dark and the smells are rich.

Oh, where have you been, Billy Boy, Billy
Boy, oh... What, you'd like to be called William?

I wanted one thing then another—always wanting.
I complained about the things I already had.

At the edge of the road, the asphalt is cracked
by the strength of daisies growing.

The wind has come up and the golden leaves fall.
I step carefully to avoid crushing insects in the dust.

I put great faith in the naked, the bare, the un-
concealed. I tell my father even though he's dead.

THIS YEAR'S WOOD

This year we cut up rotten fenceposts and old boards.
We left the fallen branches on the ground to be buried
under winter's snow. It was so easy, no setting choker
cables around logs and winching them up out of the wash
to the bank where the saw was set up. One after another,
we pulled the fenceposts off the pile and cut them. We
filled the horse trailer top to bottom and front to back.
At the house, unloading, we realized we'd cut two years'
wood. Where would we stack it? It's in the garage,
along the fence, outside the shop, beside the sheepwagon,
in the garden. There is wood everywhere. Outside, the smell
of cedar slams into me. I sit down and take a breath—one
breath after another, counting them and feeling the cedar
filling my lungs. When I am dizzy, I stand up and wobble
from woodpile to woodpile, touching each stack, thinking how
beautiful it is until I notice I am walking and forget the wood,
so equally beautiful is putting one foot in front of the other.

THE GRASS

My roof is lying on the lawn next to my house.
The golden cottonwood leaves drop down dry and crisp
onto my bed. I've folded my blankets and stacked them
in my trunk. Tired, I snuggle down into the leaves
and sleep. It is day At night the leaves tumble
down through moonlight. I have purchased a crowbar
to lever up the edge of the roof and so allow sunlight
to flood in and keep the grass alive. This is the news,
the same news they report on television, the same
triumphs and defeats, the same clear and compelling talk
whereby one is distinguished from the other. Now and
again, a late leaving bird swoops down into my room
and perches on the oak dresser that belonged to my mother.
The bird leaves its droppings there—white and gelatinous
with an edge of cloudy liquid separating from the solid.
I wrap myself happily in my clothes and watch my breath
steam against the cold mirror. I go outside, sit down
and look back in the window at my furniture and floors.
There is more to report of life as it caresses me, but I
need your help to pry up the roof and check on the grass.

The Rose Bushes

My garden is filled with the vegetables and flowers
I have planted—my cosmos and eggplant, my tomatoes,
beans, corn, marigolds, zinnias, strawberries and
raspberries, my mint, basil, chives, chilies and squash.
I eat the vegetables and they are my body. I smell
the flowers and they are both my body and what I am
that is not my body. The rose bushes I didn't plant.
I don't know who did. No one knows. My neighbors say
the roses have been here forever and the couple who
owned my house sixty years ago agrees. Roses are hardy
and have sharp barbed spines. These have survived
winters of forty below and summers of a hundred and ten.
When I arrived they were a tangled heap of brush
that didn't bloom. I cut them back and in the first
winter piled leaves and straw two feet above the ground
around them. I did this a second and third winter
and that spring there were small flowers, pink so pale
as to be white. Now they flower each year. I look at them
as I pass. I breathe deeply. They are not grateful for what
I've done and they are not mine. It is I who belong to them.

Becoming a Poet

At an anti-war demonstration I throw a stone through the floor
to ceiling windows of the Armed Forces Recruiting Office.
Years later I am waterskiing on the Zaïre River.
When the machine guns open fire, I release the rope
and drop, swimming underwater and surfacing for quick
gulps of hot air. I can hear the bullets and see the pock
of water being lifted like a flap of skin. Our boat
swoops around and I climb over the far edge. Heads below
the gunwale we turn and make another sweep to retrieve
the floating skis. It's always like this so close
to the Brazzaville side of the river. Here is the rock
in my hand. I can see the glass exploding and raining down
on the young men in their pressed uniforms. I, the pacifist,
throw my stone. Are those skis worth being shot for?
What about the boat? Do I love war? What about poetry?
This poem is a declaration of love. It starts now.

SPRING CLEANING

My daughter tells me her parents are dead. I ask if she
is all right. She says, "Yes, I painted my house pink."

The cat, waiting to pounce, stares up at the birdfeeder.
I rise from my chair, prepared to take flight.

I hang out the laundry—clean shirts and pants, underwear
and socks. Like feathers on wings, they rise in the wind.

We sat outside drinking beer, playing songs on the bottles.
Of a summer filled with days, this is the one I remember.

I leave home having forgotten a promise I made yesterday.
It was to be loving, or else to sweep the floor.

We tie on our skates and head across the ice. I watch my feet
so as not to fall, then the moon shining on my wife's head.

Windows in my house, windows in my car, windows in the buildings
and buses where I sit. I scrub and scrub trying to get them clean.

HO CHI MINH CITY

I have traveled far and around the world. Certain
distant regions belong to me as much as the house
in which I was born. I step inside and press my cheek
to its walls. The smell is always the same. Intoxicated,
I step into the night. The stars pour down on me.
I cover my head, then uncover it, and turn my face up
to swallow. The wind pushes through my long hair,
blowing it over my eyes. Later, the faint sound
of a single siren grows fainter until, straining,
I realize the whine is the earth itself, the noise caused
by friction as the planet turns against the sky. It begins
to snow. This cannot be. It is always hot in Saigon.
The flakes carry light and the darkness glows.
At first the flakes are small. I can barely see them.
By sunrise they have grown fat, falling slowly and
muffling the noise of the motorscooters in the street.
It is so quiet here, no birds sing, the butterflies and moths
have disappeared, the shining green frogs wait beneath the ice.
I am telling how the snow falls and how I can taste it, landing
on my upturned face, my tongue stretched out ardently, aflame.

MY FATHER'S DEATH

I stand up straight and toss my shoulders back.
You can do this when you are thirty. I turn and turn
and turn trying to make myself dizzy.
Unfortunately for my pleasure, I spent my youth
in the study of ballet and, reflexively, I spot.
It doesn't matter what's there in front of me—
a blossoming pear tree, a blue frozen lake,
my daughter waving and smiling from far away.
Today I gave up understanding in favor of love.
Whether or not the dead are really gone and,
if so, where to, I do not know. Still, I
cannot resist my questions and rise, walking
to the next room to see who might be there.

LEFTOVERS

My family ate leftovers. Several times a week.
What do you think—we'd throw away good food?

My neighbor throws stones at dogs who enter his yard.
He says the wind carries dandelion seeds onto his lawn.

We were sailing on a small lake in a strong wind.
Lightning struck and we were thrown into the water.

The cold war ended, Russians and Americans kept missiles
aimed at each other, not knowing what else to do.

I think of the microwave oven as a tiny dance hall,
all those particles jostling and rubbing through the night.

We are dying to be free. When it rains, some of us
dance and sing, some of us shake our fists at the sky.

This moment—perishable and fragile—we
remain inside it for all of time.

CHILDHOOD

Laughing, the three small girls run up and down the sidewalk.
They lunge for their bicycles and ride in circles in the parking lot
of the abandoned bank. One girl is dressed in blue. Another
must ride a borrowed bike. They play like this through the days
of summer. Often they come out after dinner and play some more.
The night air is shiny and soft after the dull heat of the day.
I watch them as I work in my yard, mowing and trimming the grass.
I do not long for youth. Still, there is some happiness I miss
as I hear their shouts and peals. I walk away from my garden
tools and into the house where my son sits reading a book. "You
could go outside," I say. "It would not be so bad to play there
with the neighbor girls, even though you are the only boy." He
puts down his book and leaves the room. I go in the kitchen
to have a drink of water. As I feel the liquid touch my lips,
I see the warped images of the children outside the wall. I set
the glass down and still the images dance before me, the children
and behind them the road and hills and sky circling the earth.

BOOKS

Our little house is full of books and papers.
If I have a spare minute, I sit down and scribble.
Or I find a book and begin to read. I have no fear
that my eyeballs will fall from their sockets.
I even learn new languages—doors open and behind
them are millions of books I've never seen. People say
books are a waste of time. People say poems are like
bits of broken pottery found in the ground, remnants
of some lost civilization, and did you ever think
maybe poetry had something to do with that civilization
getting lost? I smile and agree with everyone but
excuse myself as my baby daughter is calling. She wants
me to find her lost toy, or help wipe her after she pees,
or come for a walk along the creek where in winter we
stride out onto the ice. When it is thick and covered
with snow, we bend and put our ears close, listening
for the distant gurgle, the water that flows thick
and inky below us. The creek is frozen now. And so,
excuse me, but we've got to go, and I'm wondering,
as ice is to water, so is a book to what?

Before I Was Born

I floated in the belly of my mother,
blinking my eyes to look from star to star.

Near Quilcene, Washington, I saw salmon thrashing
up tiny streams, flopping out into grassy fields.

Doctors wear white smocks, or sea-green, or eggshell-blue.
If only hospitals were painted cantaloupe or strawberry or peach.

I have no fear of what others think and so
I wear a ring through my nose and let my hair grow.

Mountain, river, flower, tree. Stem, leaf,
blossom, bee. That's the letter God wrote to me.

I'm sure that I was one of twins.
He left and lives inside the moon.

I saw a deer drinking at a stream. I bent and drank
at her side until she noticed me and ran.

MY PORCH

My porch is so small there isn't room for even a chair.
The tiny roof keeps the rain off only if there is no wind,
and when it snows the white powder completely covers
the gray stone. The postman doesn't bother stepping up.
He leans across my porch to drop a letter in the box.
And when children come to ask me questions or show me
some cat or piece of metal or wound, they stay down
on the lawn and shout at me to open my door. I cross
the porch in one step and, with the injured child,
lie on the grass. We see each blade is a giant tree
under whose branches we walk protected from the storm.
And above the porch in the mountains we stand, two giants,
over spruce and fir and pine, each tree a blade of grass,
waving in the wind. Sure no one is watching, we wiggle
our fingers and let our hips sway until they touch.

ANOTHER SAIGON INTERSECTION

There is a monk who haunts me. Not the one burning,
the black human smoke rising up my nose, but the one
who is alive, the sparrow who flies into the wind,
the one who is a flower. Thirty years ago that man
sat down. What's happened since that afternoon?
I have busied myself counting the leaves that have fallen
from the cottonwood trees along the street. My father is dead.
My daughter has been born and only yesterday celebrated
her seventh birthday on this earth. I look at her
and cry. I thought I'd get used to her. My mother laughs
and tells me I never will—each day these tears of joy.

My Hope

It's always been too late for anything but love.
In spite of everything, I manage to forget.

My daughter should live to be an old woman,
and my mother regain the dream of her youth.

Counting the stars is a fine occupation,
or raindrops rolling down the windowpane.

Vietnam is hot but those nights in the jungle—rain and wind,
soaked and chilled, our teeth rattling out of our heads.

Inside the kiln it's 2400 degrees. On a brick a cricket sings.
Getting too close, my hair burns and the cricket falls silent.

It is fall and the wind is blowing. Let the children
out of school, let them chase the swirling leaves.

What exactly is my hope?
Only to see you once again.

THE POETRY OF LOVE

My gay friend tells me he has had it with the household
poets, those men writing about washing dishes, changing
the baby, mowing the grass, clipping the hedges, washing
the car, painting the bathroom, feeding the dog. "Lord
preserve us," he laughs, "from feeding the fucking dog!"
His own poems are beautiful and sad—about work and jobs,
how people in power devour people who are not. Or about
America this year—1995, our moment, and in it, the police,
the politicians, the republic of lies, the blood on the pillow,
the cracked lips, the charred skin, the blackened eyes,
the torn shirt, the broken venetian blind and the poisoned air
entering the lungs. In the same moment the poem of love:
two men lie together in bed on a long slow summer night,
the warm air touching their bodies, the feeling of languor
and excitement, the caress, the kiss. Then the reminder
that to some this love is wrong. But it is love. Another
love makes me cry when my daughter is sick with fever.
A third calls me to stop and pet the cat lying on its back
in the alley. Each love sends me spinning as when I stare
off over the edge of a mountainside. They tell us some
love is wrong, and when we wake there's a knife at our neck,
another war is in progress and thousands more are dead.

THE TREES IN MY YARD

The apple tree is over eighty years old and bears
only a few small but sweet apples each fall.
Next to it is an Englemann Spruce and in the corner
are two juniper, one planted when my father died,
the other next to it for my daughter born one month
after her grandfather's death, her placenta buried
under her tree. Under his tree, my father's spirit
waits canny and still. In front of the house
a cottonwood towers over four new aspen,
dug from the earth a few miles away and moved
to town. The weeping birch appears fragile and
the mountain ash is aflame, burning itself out in fall.
I go from tree to tree, touching each one, rubbing
my face against the various barks until my lip
is cut and blood is running both into my mouth,
and away, down the bark and onto the dry ground.

DEEP BLUE FLOWER

There's a Georgia O'Keeffe painting of clouds
in the sky, but it could be whitecaps on the sea.

The spring moist wind blows in through the open window.
Though I sleep, the coolness makes my skin tingle.

My daughter sleeps alone in her room.
I stand in the doorway and watch her breathe.

My favorite song is the one without words,
my favorite poem, the one devoid of music.

Our old Jeep is made of steel, glass, rubber and wood.
I am surprised because it seems to have a heart.

Day after day, cold. When will winter end?
The bearded iris bloom in the snow.

When I was a child a picture of Jesus hung above my bed.
My father put it there after he'd abandoned the church.

MY VILLAGE

Spring! In my village the toxic waste plant that provides jobs
has sprung a leak. Poisoned water is flowing toward the creek.
Summer! In another province a man is worn and stupefied by heat.
He rapes and murders sixteen women. After, he puts the gun
in his mouth and pulls the trigger. It misfires and he faints.
Autumn! The wind and rain swirl furiously and the leaves fall.
One soldier wakes from a dream. A second does the same. Neither
can see the other. The rockets and bombs have stopped for a
moment and the night sky, normally bright as day, has grown dark.
Winter! It is not cold at all. And the rains have stopped. In
our country this is the time of year when the children are outside.
Their bare feet slap the ground as they run over each hill
and through the town. When they see the farmer in his field,
they slip into the bush, silent, to hide. They are looking
for food. It is a melancholy world. Things are exactly
as they are. I clasp my hands before my face and give thanks.
My breath striking my thumbs is like a small distant wind,
so gentle, so sweet. This pleasure! I feel it and smile.

My Recipe

Poets name their books *Passion, Sweet Will, Iris of Creation, Blue
Autumn, Hard Country, The Beauty of the Weapons, Wordly Hopes.*

Money is so unimportant they say, so unimportant. It's your heart
that matters, your soul and humanity, your spirit, not money.

When my great aunt Alice was an old woman, she lived alone
on Hawthorne Street. Her powdered face was flat and white.

How many surrealists does it take to screw in a lightbulb?
Three: one screws in the bulb, one brings the wheelbarrow and.

I was walking down a street in a distant city. A man leapt
at me waving a knife. Not prepared to be a dead poet, I ran.

We stay up late playing scrabble. It is snowing and the windows
are dark. I think of words like "the" and "only" and "if."

Garlic, finely chopped onion, cumin, cardamon, red chiles, orange,
cinnamon, black mustard, cilantro. That's the secret of my recipe.

HALLOWEEN

The children run from house to house. Halloween night
with plastic flashlights. Some break or fade as batteries
wear down. The chemical lightsticks glow when struck
against a hard surface. After six hours they too fade.
There is a knock at the door and my neighbor's son,
dressed as a nineteenth century French convict, says, "Trick
or Treat." He looks down and seems embarrassed or ashamed.
I hand the plate of cookies to him. My wife made them this
morning. We sat together writing our name and phone number
on thin slips of paper. We put one of these with each cookie
and wrapped both in clear plastic. A junior high girl
dressed as a witch looks up at me and says, "You didn't
put poison in these, did you?" "No." I say. "Or LSD?"
No again. "Too bad." She jokes. She giggles. She can't
stop. The giggle becomes a laugh. She stands facing me
on the tiny porch and laughs and laughs. I do, too. When
she stops, it is to ask, "Did you ever take LSD?" I wipe
the tears from my eyes, unsure what I should say.

My Sleep

We lay in our sleeping bags on the capitol steps
in Salem, Oregon, protesting the Vietnam war.
The candles shone in the darkness, flickering
under the red and blue lights of the state police.
It was raining and we shivered in our wet bags,
our long hair shining around our young faces.
Someone started singing. There was laughter.
We ate cheap hamburgers cooked by someone not
with us and we drank cheap red wine and smoked dope.
The war was far away as we blew out the candles.
The thin streams of smoke floated noisily away.
I couldn't sleep—partly because of the war
and partly because I longed to make love but
I had no one to make love with. Now I know
I should have made love with the soldier,
the boy I went to high school with who wasn't
at college. When he came home, I should have
taken him in my arms. How did we get so tired,
and so still? But my soldier had rotten feet and
there was dried blood around his eyes. He rolled
out his government issue sleeping bag and lay down
beside me. I wrapped my long hair around my face
and began walking alone to Vietnam. That brother
handed me a gun and explained how to use it. Each
of us knows what the other did. There is a barking
dog who reminds us and candles we do not light
and children who play in the warm streets and the war
beginning again after a night of silent harmless sleep.

THE END OF THE CENTURY

We are coming soon to the end of the century.
I see it shining in the trees across the street.

Many of us have been beaten up. We lie with blackened eyes
and bloodied noses. We scream the names of those we blame.

My father was a carpenter. He died and left me a hand drill
and steel bits. I built a playhouse for my daughter.

They give us paradise and we are asked to fly, but our wings
are of paper or ash, our heads of lead and our bodies of stone.

If you hold my hand, I will forgive you. We can dig our car
out of the snow. What do you mean I was the one driving?

Adolf Hitler is born and dies. He returns as the President of
Iran or South Africa or the US. Reincarnation is running wild.

Let's go to the movies. Buildings and airplanes explode into flame.
We can avert our eyes and kiss in the flickering orange light.

My Basement

In a damp corner of the basement I set up my room, painting
the gray cement walls white. It was hard forcing the paint
into the dark stony holes—a deep grotto, a Spanish cave
I painted with animals—thundering bison twisted in anger
and pain, spears jammed into their necks and shoulders;
deer surrounded by wolves, each wolf leaping high into the air,
jaws open but ready to close; above both scenes small birds,
fluttering and singing. I felt faint, but it could have been
the paint fumes trapped underground. When I looked around I saw
the washing machine and the green enamel gas stove we are saving
and the poster that says this basement is a nuclear free zone.
I heard steps on the floor above me then the toilet flushing,
the waste water pouring down the pipes. I stood up to clear
my head and walked into the other half of the basement where
I sat down on the tool box my father left me when he died.
Though the metal is battered and gray, inside the tools shine—
two sharp saws, the brace and bits, plumb bob, nail punch,
level and square. Sparkling steel and fine polished wood.
I picked up the tools and held them in my paint-covered hands.

SIXTY

On her sixtieth birthday my mother-in-law's friends give her a card
with a picture of a floozy on the front. The floozy has hair dyed
red. She is smoking a cigarette in a diamond holder and wearing
a negligee which is both see-through and support. Her breasts
are pushed up tight against one another so they appear close
and large. She smiles a wicked smile and says, "Want to look
young on your birthday?" Inside the card is written, "Go braless,
it'll pull the wrinkles out of your face." My mother-in-law looks
quietly at the card. When she opens it and reads the punch line,
she laughs. She covers her mouth and laughs again, shyly then
loudly. She says, "Wait till you see this," and passes the card
around the room to her friends. She opens her presents. With each
one, no matter if it is elegant, tasteless, rare, or dumb, she thanks
the giver, graciously and sincerely. She happily takes the next
package. I watch in silence. She is a beautiful woman, a girl,
sprawled on the floor, her arms and legs and her eyes, like a
waterfall that tumbles, enveloping us all.

THE BIGGEST FISH

I go out fishing, crossing oceans, lakes, rivers and streams.
I row and row and find I like it and there's no time to fish.

My nephew has a dust collection. He keeps it in a variety
of colored glass jars that he polishes each morning with a rag.

Wood, natural gas, methane, coal, uranium, oil, wax, the flesh
of whales, wind, water, sun. All these fuels and never enough.

The two-step is a fine dance. So is the polka, the huapango,
chotis, cumbia, vals. You could spend your life dancing.

On very hot days it is possible to remain cool—
bury yourself in the earth and wait for night.

"How many marbles you got in that bag, boy?" the man asked me.
"I don't know." I said, and fell to the ground to count them.

For years I've been hunting for the right religion—in Peru,
Hopiland, Japan, Rome. I can't just embrace anything.

THE WINDMILL

I pull on the dark coveralls and climb the delicate ladder.
At the top I pull myself onto the narrow platform
and clip the heavy safety harness around the steel shaft.
I take a wrench from my pocket and remove the tin plate
covering the oilpan. The cogged wheels rest, partially
submerged in their bath of graying oil. I drain this oil
into a bucket and lower it with a rope to the ground.
As I pour in fresh oil the wind rises. Though the rotor
blades are locked they try to turn and the assembly
swings around threatening to knock me into space.
I lean against the mill and pour. The wind catches
the stream of oil making it fly in long looping threads.
Where it lands it will kill the grass. Back on earth
I release the brake and the blades spin, singing in the wind.
The water spills into the stock tank. It is pure and clear,
and so, gratefully, I cup my greasy hands and drink.

My Death

I didn't die there in Vietnam amidst the whistles
and shrieks, nor in loud Zaïre, the tiny bullets
being swallowed by the blue green beautiful river,
the water pulled by the hot wind into the hotter sky.
In Kampala, the man who pushed his pistol through the window
of my sky blue VW Bug thought better of it, or hesitated
as I sped away through broken cement under the smiles
of beer drinkers leaning out of slashed billboards.
Those hooded figures in the night who rose from behind
the ridge and threw me face down in the sand, my death
felt pretty near then, the implement of its execution
pressed into the pale skin of my neck. What will fate
think of next? There are the thousands of more ordinary
escapes and bruisings—mishaps in automobiles and airplanes,
sickness, lost once in the mountains in the cold, more.
It is not so much that I wonder how I will die, or when,
or even if, perhaps, I've died already and, as they say,
this might be heaven or it might be hell. What I want
to know is, what I want to know is, just a minute, it's
on the tip of my tongue, excuse me, wait, just a minute.

FLYING FISH

In October, far from our already cold Wyoming home,
my daughter and I walk along the shore. The air is hot
and the water warm. We play in the surf. When we are tired,
we sit on the sand watching the waves break. In each crest
something shimmers and sparkles—thousands of fish rolling
in the green. It is night and we are on a train, rushing
through the dark, slowing only as we enter a town.
On the platform, a single light breaks the darkness
and we glimpse a face, a hand rising to wave,
then both are gone and we thunder back into the dark.
One fish flips languorously and, briefly, somehow, slowly,
in a dreamy lazy way, rises to the surface. A pelican
plummets and strikes, lifting the fish whose gills snap
and suck against the thin air. We feel sad for the fish,
who makes its journey but once. We feel sad for the bird,
making the same journey day after day. My daughter leaps
into the water and cupping her hands just so, begins to swim.

WHEN I DECIDE

When I became a conscientious objector to war
my father was torn—his country or his son.

Those evangelists at my door are angels.
It doesn't matter if the message is garbled.

In the Peace Corps they vaccinated us against hepatitis,
cholera, small pox, rabies, only forgetting to close our eyes.

Everything we've known we still know.
This includes good things as well as bad.

I wondered and wondered if I'd ever have an original
thought. Then I did and was frightened to death.

In the garden the plants crest the waves of warming soil.
I push my hands into the darkness but can't forget this poem.

There is a seed pod floating outside my window.
A several thousand pound saguaro is learning to fly.

COMMERCE

For a time in Saigon everyone wanted to be a monk.
Citizens traded their suits for salmon colored robes
sewn in Hong Kong mills. Fine china saucers became
begging bowls. The city, which had been falling apart,
now hung securely by a thread. The blink of a bird's eye
would cause more destruction than the American president
with his headaches and bad moods and bowel obstructions
following sleepless nights. I look out on my lawn
and see soldiers. So many soldiers! The grass is long
and needs mowing. The clipped pieces fly into the wind.
Where they land, soldiers rise, fully armed if poorly
trained. I turn away from the mower and rub my hands
through my hair. I see it is coming out in clumps.
I'm nervous, going bald. I shake the hair from my hand
and where it lands more soldiers rise—every hair
on every person has fallen out—the hair on our heads
and necks, our armpit hairs, pubic hairs, nostril hairs.
Against my will, I am breeding soldiers in my garden
and within my body. I rush into the house to order more
robes from Hong Kong. "You again," the voice on the phone
says, "Every ten or twenty years, your emergency order.
So what'll it be, the soldiers or the monks?" "Well,"
I say, "I don't know." And when I hang up, I see the bird
waiting to blink and the saucers piled high with food
and the sun and moon shining, waiting for me to decide.

MY STOOP

On a February day, I sat on the cold cement step
in front of my house and watched the silent traffic,
the frozen clouds, the skeletal bushes in the yard.
February—a friend calls it a shitty, little month.
But Feburary is not a shitty little month. February
is nothing at all. Surprised, I notice I love this life
and this quiet out of the way place. It's hard to admit
that I have changed, that what I wanted was perhaps
not the thing to want, or that wanting itself was not
so much the wrong way home as simply the roundabout way.
Even though I am wearing wool pants, the cold seeps through.
When I stand I see the morning sun shining on the green
roof across the street. In the warmth, the melting snow
leaves wet streaks, long lines an even darker green.

ONCE UPON A TIME

Once upon a time there was a complicated story
dealing with umbrellas, surgery and nuclear weapons.

Everywhere the cities grow larger and larger.
They fill the entire planet with their news.

There is a French expression—*mal dans sa peau*. It means
to be uncomfortable in your skin, like an ill fitting suit.

Nowadays almost no one owns phonograph records.
I keep mine in memory of the past.

The first woman I loved left me. I fell to the floor sobbing.
Looking back, I also remember the dust floating in the light.

Late one night a hit and run driver killed my dog. A teenaged
boy found her and sat on the sidewalk holding her bleeding body.

All stories have an ending. Usually
it is, "and things went on."

My Art

It is eternity with whom I play, the long swell and rise
I call forever and the way I imagine I can be a part of it
and never die. I call death to my side and say, "Sit with me."
And death sits. He is a man. She is a woman. Death's face
can be anything I need. A red rose floats where Death's face
used to be. I kick my chair away and float with the rose.
I take a pencil and write down some words that will give me
eternal life. Any words will do. Even casually spoken ones.
When I open my mouth the words that come out never disappear.
They fly across the galaxies and land in God's ear. God says,
"I've known that forever. Still, it's nice to hear from you."

Windows

Twelve windows. And the doors! Each is also a window.
In one the glass is chemically etched to show a stag,
a doe and two fawns browsing in a wooded glade.
This tableau is framed by a wide floral border
opening onto a covered porch where we watch the rain.
The double French doors, each with ten small panes
of glass, swing open onto a small uncovered deck
built in the shape of a grand piano. We sit here
when it is sunny and warm. In the kitchen door
is a leaded glass portrait of a man sleeping—
partly on his side, partly on his stomach.
One arm is bent over his head, one leg pulled up
toward his ribs, his testicles close against him.
I almost forgot! There is another window—deep blue
etched to show the violent ocean. White foaming waves
scud along and in the spray the poet Denise Levertov's
words warn that, "as you read, the sea is turning
its dark pages, turning its dark pages." This is
the window where I like to sit. But I do not read.
There is my sister-in-law trudging heavily down the street,
a cloud of sorrow billowing out from her clothes and settling
on each blade of grass. There are the two thin neighbor girls.
No matter the sadness of their household, they run laughing
along the street, shouting and waving at each person who passes.
Our border collie Cleo stands in the middle of the road.
Once again I see her startled look as the car slams into her,
and keeps going. It is not as though only bitter thoughts arise
at this window. I admit I personally am happy. And if I smash
the glass, the force of the universe will suck me out of the house,
and I will careen away, arms and legs going every direction at once.

MY CABIN

I return to my cabin along the shore. Once far from any
neighbor, now it is surrounded by houses and cars.
I can hear rock and roll music. The noise is deafening
and electric and soon I am snapping my fingers, a thousand
fingers and each pair snapping. Bang! My cabin flies
away to Wyoming where it sits slightly crooked below
Cloud Peak in the Bighorn Range. Surrounded by a thousand
acres of trees and wildflowers, the only music is the whuuuu
of the wind in the tops of the spruce and pine. My neighbors
are snapping their fingers so I can relax and bend to pick
flowers for my table. At sunset my horse walks away
into a nearby grove where I can't see him. The sound of
breaking twigs and branches tells me where he grazes.
When the moon comes up its light strikes the silver rivets
on his bridle and reflects from there to my eyes. I walk
to where he waits and pull myself up onto his back.
I feel weak even though I am strong. My cabin settles
crooked on the hillside. The neighbors are clouds
and trees. So many years have gone by and still
the bright wildflowers are fresh in their dark vase.

This High Mountain

This high mountain—above the treeline, rocks and lichens.
In June we boulder hop to still-frozen lakes.

The Pacific Ocean, vast and distant. Here at the shore
where the water meets the land, it is mine.

I feel far from our world of technology. Against my better
judgment I wish there were no cars, computers, asphalt or glass.

This could tangle a person up, this fifty foot extension cord
left lying under the snow. What happens in April's thaw?

At age ten, my dream was to be an astronaut,
to go to some living planet unlike our own.

Now I am a man. On my desk there is a single fall flower
alive in a raku vase. The flower is magenta, yellow and black.

I have found the great loves of my life—
prairie, mountain, sky, my daughter and my wife.

Twenty-Five Cents

When I am reborn I will know that I have lived
another life. My infant daughter has told me.
She remembers things that I claim never happened—
the fire, for example, in the barn, the flames,
and the time the horse ran away with her and she was
afraid she would fall but she clung to the mane.
In answer to all my questions beginning with "Why?"
she answers, "Because the birds are sleeping, and
when they wake up they fly." She has convinced me
that on the day when I wake up, I, too, will fly.
I will traverse the globe dressed in a suit and tie,
striving to help others elevate their material lives.
And whether I fall into ruin and have nothing to give,
or am killed in a freak accident, or change my mind,
I'll go on—the coins in my pocket will clatter
noisily to the ground and someone will pick them up.

My Lesson

In the flower bed below the open window, iris and day-lilies
grow. The iris bloom early and as the last of them fades,
the day lilies come on—fiery yellow and orange replacing
Japanese blue and Swahili black. In spring, when the ground
begins to thaw, I break the iris apart. Working like this
in the dirt, my happiness is deep and rich. The frail spring
sun strikes the back of my neck and head. I fall over backwards
and throw my arms out from my sides, staring up at the pale
blue sky. I think I could not bear beauty greater than this,
but when I turn my head, there is more. I pull a little dirt
from the ground and crumble it into my mouth. Suddenly I think
of Vietnam—twenty years and more ago, yet waiting for me,
timeless and new. Vietnam and the flowers, together every day.

POLITICS

Victim goes on shooting spree!
Prosecutor pleads Not Guilty.

I live at the base of an ancient and stunning mountain range.
I long for the ocean, the waves beating at the shore.

The candidate refuses to divulge his platform or beliefs.
"It would only confuse the issue," he reveals.

When it stopped snowing, I went out and shoveled the path.
Left to itself, Spring would have done my job.

The sun goes down and a hundred million television sets come on.
The blue glow is beautiful in the dark.

We know when the rainy season comes. Still, year after year,
we secretly hope, when it's dry, the droplets will fall.

Is Mahatma Gandhi the world's greatest politician?
Or is he telling the truth?

TRAFFIC

My house is pale blue and on Main Street. At night
the cars race up and down as if they were a storm.
Every night they go faster and their drivers grow younger.
No matter how much cotton I stuff in my ears, the news
of my town comes to me—the man who beat his wife and
molested his daughter, the alcoholic parents and children
and cousins and friends, the plan to cut down one more
tree to make room for a building and build one more road
to escape this town. I have decided to go outside and
sit on the small deck shaped like a piano that I built
myself. I take my old socks and a needle and thread,
and begin to darn. The sun shines on my face and warms
it slightly but at twenty below it is never enough
and I am cold. When the sun sets it will be colder
and too dark for me to go on with my darning. Then I will
lean back and watch the moon rise. Nodding, I am startled
by the sound of tires screeching on the street. The jolt
makes me jump and I prick my finger with the needle. It
hurts for only a moment and is not deep enough to bleed.

THE ICE

Warm days and cold nights—ice everywhere.
The black asphalt of the road shines through it.
Glassy mountain ranges push upward below the eaves.
The short walk from the house to the shop has become
a treacherous journey. With each new snow, the slick
polished ice is briefly gone, but it returns and winter
is ever more clearly a mirror. Who wants all of life
to be so obvious? In the cold and dark we sink deeper
into our reflections. It is depressing how many faults
we have. Oh, well, we're still like other people, wanting
to be in love so much that we love each other in spite of
ourselves. Why not? One evening, when the air is still,
we walk to the pond and put on our skates. There's the mayor
and her husband, the school teachers and all the kids,
the grocer, the priest, hey, wait, everyone in town is here,
skating furiously around on the ice, watching their feet
which means they are not watching the other skaters
and so constantly collide with them and are forced
to throw their arms around each other to stay upright.

MY LEGACY

When I am gone, what will remain of me on this earth?
The garden I have worked in year by year, the flowers
and the volunteer vegetables that appear in such
unlikely spots each spring—the lettuce and spinach
and parsley poking out from under late spring's snow,
where last year there was tomato or squash or corn.
In a few years the garden will be only a jumble
of weeds and dying vines. There are the two rooms
I built for our house, the wide windows thrown open
on summer evenings and the stars that come spinning
down through the Wyoming dark sky. These will last
a little longer, but soon they too will be a jumble
of unrecognizable wood and stone. All this matter—
it disappears. Still, I am not sad. I'll be here,
my memory floating like a leaf on Clear Creek, and
the gurgle of the water as it spins dizzyingly along.

UNBELIEVABLE

1919, my father was born somewhere in Idaho, a river flowed
by his house—the Snake or maybe it was the Coeur d'Alene.

Five people shrunk onto a postcard pinned above my desk,
but they are only strangers—I don't pretend they are my family.

I wash the dishes then sweep the floor, do laundry and
chop wood. Finally I take pen in hand to say this.

Last night the moon over the lake, the temperature forty below,
everything shimmering as if in that moment being born.

A deer floated through the woods. It flew. And look—
no hoofprints but a wingbeat traced in the snow.

I thought shooting stars really were stars off the track.
Why not our earth? I asked with a shudder and a smile.

Love conquers all. And so I curl up in church,
believing every unbelievable word the priest can say.

MEDITATION

We sat under the madrona trees in the light rain that swirled
around us and up our noses with the air we breathed.
My legs were folded before me and the back of one hand rested
in the palm of the other, my thumbs touching lightly,
barely grazing one another so that a slight electric current
flowed through me in a circle. It shocked me to think
we were sitting under the beautiful madronas in order to stop
the first nuclear submarine from arriving in our homeland.
Doubtful, I was doubly shocked when I realized it would work.
I remembered other beautiful trees and other homelands
and Vietnam. I was never there. A muddy path circled
the half ruined sheds of a formerly secure village.
At dawn, the clouds rolled and, as if for the first time,
it rained. The largest building was only a wooden floor
hung from poles, a long rectangle with walls on three sides.
The monks were seated in two rows, facing one another.
The rain came harder and harder from the open side of the room.
With no guidelines, I thought of the absent wall and why
it faced the pounding rain, the silent drenched monks.
I waved my arms around my face, showing the rain hitting us all
and us all shivering and why? Why sit there in such discomfort?
Why stay? Aware that a gentleman removes his hat when indoors,
I took my helmet off and water poured to the floor. They
said it was a strange day, that rain never came from the open
side of the building. Oh, I said, and feeling a little better,
I picked up my wet helmet and placed it atop my steaming head.

Who Owes Us

No one owes us anything.
We claim it's mother and father.

How can you live in this place?
The floors are so dirty and it stinks.

I sit waiting for the mailman. There's a package
he's bringing. Why isn't he here yet?

The worm is alive. The apple tree, the coyote, the walnut,
the beggar, the oilman, the stone and the dust and the sky.

If a man or woman finds nothing in work, it is time to retire.
Or find something new. Surely God is not tired of his job.

It is so pleasant to look into the empty bucket, the velvety
dark space. If you have to, cut a hole in the metal bottom.

I am a lecturer in the university. My students sleep
through my talks but wake up in time for the tests.